The Merchant of Venice

By William Shakespeare

Abridged for Schools and Performance

By KJ O'Hara

Copyright © 2015 by KJ O'Hara

The right of KJ O'Hara to identify himself as adapter of this work is asserted by him under accordance of the Copyright, Designs and Patents Act, 1988

All rights reserved. Except as permitted under current legislation, no part of this work may be photocopied, stored in a retrieval system, published, performed in public, adapted, broadcast, transmitted, recorded or reproduced in any form by any means without prior permission of the copyright holder.
Permission for and licence to perform this version in public can be obtained from the address at the bottom of this page.

First Published 2015

Cover Illustration Copyright © Ruchela

Although the adapter and publisher have made every effort to ensure that the information in this book was correct at press time, the adapter and publisher do not assume and hereby disclaim any liability to any party for any loss, damage, or disruption caused by errors or omissions, whether such errors or omissions result from negligence, accident, or any other cause.

ISBN: 978-1517582876
Published by Antic Mind
102 Dudwell Lane, Halifax, UK. HX30SH
All Enquiries to publisher@anticmind.com

Contents

Forward 7
Dramatis Personae 8
ACT I SCENE I 9
ACT I SCENE II 13
ACT I SCENE III 17
ACT II SCENE I 23
ACT II SCENE II 24
ACT II SCENE III 28
ACT II SCENE IV 29
ACT II SCENE V 31
ACT II SCENE VI 33
ACT II SCENE VII 35
ACT II SCENE VIII 37
ACT II SCENE IX 39
ACT III SCENE I 42
ACT III SCENE II 46
ACT III SCENE III 54
ACT III SCENE IV 56
ACT IV SCENE I 58
ACT IV SCENE II 72
ACT V SCENE I 73

Forward

In abridging The Merchant of Venice for schools and performance I have brought together my experience as former Artistic Director of Antic Mind Theatre Company and of being an English and drama teacher for over 20 years.

The aim was to produce a shortened version which would improve the accessibility of the play to a younger audience and, at the same time, thoroughly engage them in this thought-provoking and intriguing plot. In doing so, I have ensured that the essential elements of the play remain fully intact: the plot is coherent, characters are developed and all the text is original. In that sense it still contains everything an English teacher would want to see in an abridged version: key speeches and parts of scenes that teachers would want to focus on in lessons have been left alone and I've not cut anything which I thought would be useful for studying the underlying themes in the play.

The abridgement required only one shorter scene to be removed in its entirety; the main revisions have been to cut extraneous dialogue from scenes. This was done partially to allow the play to be performed by a small cast and partially to make it more streamlined and, therefore, easier for a young audience to understand and follow.

As a drama teacher, I have used this version of the text many times with my students. Sometimes we have used it for exploration, at others it has been used as a script for performance. I have even used it as the basis to make even shorter abridgements for students to perform in small groups as examination pieces.

This version allows drama teachers the flexibility to perform the play with a large or small number of students.

KJ O'Hara

Dramatis Personae

THE DUKE OF VENICE

PRINCE OF MOROCCO and PRINCE OF ARRAGON, Suitors to Portia

ANTONIO, a Merchant of Venice

BASSANIO, his Friend

GRATIANO, SALANIO, & SALARINO: Friends to Antonio and Bassanio

LORENZO, in love with Jessica

SHYLOCK, a rich Jew

TUBAL, a Jew, his Friend

LAUNCELOT GOBBO, Servant to Shylock

OLD GOBBO, Father to Launcelot

LEONARDO, Servant to Bassanio

BALTHASAR Servant to Portia

PORTIA, a rich Heiress

NERISSA, her Waiting-maid

JESSICA, Daughter to Shylock

ACT I SCENE I

A street in Venice

Enter ANTONIO, SALARINO, and SALANIO

ANTONIO   In sooth, I know not why I am so sad:
It wearies me; you say it wearies you;
But how I caught it, found it, or came by it,
What stuff 'tis made of, whereof it is born,
I am to learn.

SALARINO   Your mind is tossing on the ocean;
There, where your argosies with portly sail,
Like signiors and rich burghers on the flood,
Do overpeer the petty traffickers,
As they fly by them with their woven wings.

SALANIO   Believe me, sir, had I such venture forth,
The better part of my affections would
Be with my hopes abroad. I should be still
Plucking the grass, to know where sits the wind,
Peering in maps for ports and piers and roads;
And every object that might make me fear
Misfortune to my ventures, out of doubt
Would make me sad.

SALARINO   I know, Antonio
Is sad to think upon his merchandise.

ANTONIO   Believe me, no: I thank my fortune for it,
My ventures are not in one bottom trusted,
Nor to one place; nor is my whole estate
Upon the fortune of this present year:
Therefore my merchandise makes me not sad.

SALARINO   Why, then you are in love.

ANTONIO   Fie, fie!

SALARINO Not in love neither? Then let us say you are sad,
Because you are not merry: and 'twere as easy
For you to laugh and leap and say you are merry,
Because you are not sad.

Enter BASSANIO, LORENZO, and GRATIANO

SALANIO Here comes Bassanio, your most noble kinsman,
Gratiano and Lorenzo. Fare ye well:
We leave you now with better company.

SALARINO Good morrow, my good lords.

Exeunt Salarino and Salanio

LORENZO My Lord Bassanio, since you have found Antonio,
We two will leave you: but at dinner-time,
I pray you, have in mind where we must meet.

BASSANIO I will not fail you.

GRATIANO You look not well, Signior Antonio;
You have too much respect upon the world:
They lose it that do buy it with much care:
Believe me, you are marvellously changed.

ANTONIO I hold the world but as the world, Gratiano;
A stage where every man must play a part,
And mine a sad one.

GRATIANO Let me play the fool:
With mirth and laughter let old wrinkles come,
And let my liver rather heat with wine
Than my heart cool with mortifying groans.
Come, good Lorenzo. Fare ye well awhile.

LORENZO Well, we will leave you then till dinner-time.

ANTONIO Farewell.

Exeunt GRATIANO and LORENZO

ANTONIO Well, tell me now what lady is the same
To whom you swore a secret pilgrimage,
That you to-day promised to tell me of?

BASSANIO 'Tis not unknown to you, Antonio,
How much I have disabled mine estate,
By something showing a more swelling port
Than my faint means would grant continuance:
Nor do I now make moan to be abridged
From such a noble rate; but my chief care
Is to come fairly off from the great debts
Wherein my time something too prodigal
Hath left me gaged. To you, Antonio,
I owe the most, in money and in love,
And from your love I have a warranty
To unburden all my plots and purposes
How to get clear of all the debts I owe.

ANTONIO I pray you, good Bassanio, let me know it;
And if it stand, as you yourself still do,
Within the eye of honour, be assured,
My purse, my person, my extremest means,
Lie all unlock'd to your occasions.

BASSANIO In my school-days, when I had lost one shaft,
I shot his fellow of the self-same flight
The self-same way with more advised watch,
To find the other forth, and by adventuring both
I oft found both: I urge this childhood proof,
Because what follows is pure innocence.
I owe you much, and, like a wilful youth,
That which I owe is lost; but if you please
To shoot another arrow that self way
Which you did shoot the first, I do not doubt,
As I will watch the aim, or to find both
Or bring your latter hazard back again
And thankfully rest debtor for the first.

ANTONIO   You know me well, do but say to me what I should do
That in your knowledge may by me be done,
And I am prest unto it: therefore, speak.

BASSANIO   In Belmont is a lady richly left;
And she is fair, and, fairer than that word,
Of wondrous virtues: sometimes from her eyes
I did receive fair speechless messages:
Her name is Portia, nothing undervalued
To Cato's daughter, Brutus' Portia:
Nor is the wide world ignorant of her worth,
For the four winds blow in from every coast
Renowned suitors, and her sunny locks
Hang on her temples like a golden fleece;
And many Jasons come in quest of her.
O my Antonio, had I but the means
To hold a rival place with one of them,
I have a mind presages me such thrift,
That I should questionless be fortunate!

ANTONIO   Thou know'st that all my fortunes are at sea;
Neither have I money nor commodity
To raise a present sum: therefore go forth;
Try what my credit can in Venice do:
That shall be rack'd, even to the uttermost,
To furnish thee to Belmont, to fair Portia.
Go, presently inquire, and so will I,
Where money is, and I no question make
To have it of my trust or for my sake.

Exeunt

ACT I SCENE II

Belmont. A room in PORTIA'S house.

Enter PORTIA and NERISSA

PORTIA By my troth, Nerissa, my little body is aweary of
this great world.

NERISSA You would be, sweet madam, if your miseries were in
the same abundance as your good fortunes are: and
yet, for aught I see, they are as sick that surfeit
with too much as they that starve with nothing.

PORTIA Good sentences and well pronounced.

NERISSA They would be better, if well followed.

PORTIA It is a good divine that follows his own instructions:
I can easier teach twenty what were good
to be done, than be one of the twenty to
follow mine own teaching. The brain may
devise laws for the blood, but a hot temper leaps
o'er a cold decree: but this reasoning is not in the fashion to
choose me a husband. O me, the word 'choose!' I may
neither choose whom I would nor refuse whom I
dislike; so is the will of a living daughter curbed
by the will of a dead father. Is it not hard,
Nerissa, that I cannot choose one nor refuse none?

NERISSA Your father was ever virtuous; and holy men at their
death have good inspirations: therefore the lottery,
that he hath devised in these three chests of gold,
silver and lead, whereof who chooses his meaning
chooses you, will, no doubt, never be chosen by any
rightly but one who shall rightly love. But what
warmth is there in your affection towards any of
these princely suitors that are already come?

PORTIA I pray thee, over-name them; and as thou namest them, I will describe them; and, according to my description, level at my affection.

NERISSA First, there is the Neapolitan prince.

PORTIA Ay, that's a colt indeed, for he doth nothing but talk of his horse; and he makes it a great appropriation to his own good parts, that he can shoe him himself. I am much afeard my lady his mother played false with a smith.

NERISSA Then there is the County Palatine.

PORTIA He doth nothing but frown, he hears merry tales and smiles not: I fear he will prove the weeping philosopher when he grows old, being so full of unmannerly sadness in his youth. I had rather be married to a death's-head with a bone in his mouth than to either of these. God defend me from these two!

NERISSA How say you by the French lord, Monsieur Le Bon?

PORTIA God made him, and therefore let him pass for a man. In truth, I know it is a sin to be a mocker: but, he! why, he hath a horse better than the Neapolitan's, a better bad habit of frowning than the Count Palatine; he is every man in no man: he will fence with his own shadow: if I should marry him, I should marry twenty husbands. If he would despise me I would forgive him, for if he love me to madness, I shall never requite him.

NERISSA What say you, then, to Falconbridge, the young baron of England?

PORTIA You know I say nothing to him, for he understands not me, nor I him: he hath neither Latin, French,

	nor Italian, and you will come into the court and swear that I have a poor pennyworth in the English. He is a proper man's picture, but, alas, who can converse with a dumb-show? How oddly he is suited! I think he bought his doublet in Italy, his round hose in France, his bonnet in Germany and his behaviour everywhere.
NERISSA	What think you of the Scottish lord, his neighbour?
PORTIA	That he hath a neighbourly charity in him, for he borrowed a box of the ear of the Englishman and swore he would pay him again when he was able: I think the Frenchman became his surety and sealed under for another.
NERISSA	How like you the young German, the Duke of Saxony's nephew?
PORTIA	Very vilely in the morning, when he is sober, and most vilely in the afternoon, when he is drunk: when he is best, he is a little worse than a man, and when he is worst, he is little better than a beast: and the worst fall that ever fell, I hope I shall make shift to go without him.
NERISSA	If he should offer to choose, and choose the right casket, you should refuse to perform your father's will, if you should refuse to accept him.
PORTIA	Therefore, for fear of the worst, I pray thee, set a deep glass of rhenish wine on the contrary casket, for if the devil be within and that temptation without, I know he will choose it. I will do any thing, Nerissa, ere I'll be married to a sponge.
NERISSA	You need not fear, lady, the having any of these lords: they have acquainted me with their determinations; which is, indeed, to return to their home and to trouble you with no more suit, unless

	you may be won by some other sort than your father's imposition depending on the caskets.
PORTIA	If I live to be as old as Sibylla, I will die as chaste as Diana, unless I be obtained by the manner of my father's will.
NERISSA	Do you not remember, lady, in your father's time, a Venetian, a scholar and a soldier, that came hither in company of the Marquis of Montferrat?
PORTIA	Yes, yes, it was Bassanio; as I think, he was so called.
NERISSA	True, madam: he, of all the men that ever my foolish eyes looked upon, was the best deserving a fair lady.
PORTIA	I remember him well, and I remember him worthy of thy praise.

Enter a Serving-man

	How now! what news?
Servant	The four strangers seek for you, madam, to take their leave: and there is a forerunner come from a fifth, the Prince of Morocco, who brings word the prince his master will be here to-night.
PORTIA	If I could bid the fifth welcome with so good a heart as I can bid the other four farewell, I should be glad of his approach: if he have the condition of a saint and the complexion of a devil, I had rather he should shrive me than wive me. Come, Nerissa. Sirrah, go before. Whiles we shut the gates upon one wooer, another knocks at the door.

Exeunt

ACT I SCENE III

Venice. A public place.

Enter BASSANIO and SHYLOCK

SHYLOCK Three thousand ducats; well.

BASSANIO Ay, sir, for three months.

SHYLOCK For three months; well.

BASSANIO For the which, as I told you, Antonio shall be bound.

SHYLOCK Three thousand ducats for three months and Antonio bound.

BASSANIO Your answer to that.

SHYLOCK Antonio is a good man.

BASSANIO Have you heard any imputation to the contrary?

SHYLOCK Oh, no, no, no, no: my meaning in saying he is a good man is to have you understand me that he is sufficient. Yet his means are in supposition: he hath an argosy bound to Tripolis, another to the Indies; I understand moreover, upon the Rialto, he hath a third at Mexico, a fourth for England, and other ventures he hath, squandered abroad. But ships are but boards, sailors but men: there be land-rats and water-rats, water-thieves and land-thieves, I mean pirates, and then there is the peril of waters, winds and rocks. The man is, notwithstanding, sufficient. Three thousand ducats; I think I may take his bond.

BASSANIO Be assured you may.

SHYLOCK I will be assured I may; and, that I may be assured,
I will bethink me. May I speak with Antonio?

BASSANIO If it please you to dine with us.

SHYLOCK Yes, to smell pork; to eat of the habitation which
your prophet the Nazarite conjured the devil into. I
will buy with you, sell with you, talk with you,
walk with you, and so following, but I will not eat
with you, drink with you, nor pray with you. What
news on the Rialto? Who is he comes here?

Enter ANTONIO

BASSANIO This is Signior Antonio.

SHYLOCK [Aside] How like a fawning publican he looks!
I hate him for he is a Christian,
But more for that in low simplicity
He lends out money gratis and brings down
The rate of usance here with us in Venice.
If I can catch him once upon the hip,
I will feed fat the ancient grudge I bear him.
He hates our sacred nation, and he rails,
Even there where merchants most do congregate,
On me, my bargains and my well-won thrift,
Which he calls interest. Cursed be my tribe,
If I forgive him!

BASSANIO Shylock, do you hear?

SHYLOCK I am debating of my present store,
And, by the near guess of my memory,
I cannot instantly raise up the gross
Of full three thousand ducats. What of that?
Tubal, a wealthy Hebrew of my tribe,
Will furnish me. But soft! how many months
Do you desire?

To ANTONIO Rest you fair, good signior;
Your worship was the last man in our mouths.

ANTONIO   Shylock, although I neither lend nor borrow
By taking nor by giving of excess,
Yet, to supply the ripe wants of my friend,
I'll break a custom. Is he yet possess'd
How much ye would?

SHYLOCK   Ay, ay, three thousand ducats.

ANTONIO   And for three months.

SHYLOCK   I had forgot; three months; you told me so.
Well then, your bond; and let me see; but hear you;
Methought you said you neither lend nor borrow
Upon advantage.

ANTONIO   I do never use it.

SHYLOCK   When Jacob grazed his uncle Laban's sheep--
This Jacob from our holy Abram was,
As his wise mother wrought in his behalf,
The third possessor; ay, he was the third--

ANTONIO   And what of him? did he take interest?

SHYLOCK   No, not take interest, not, as you would say,
Directly interest: mark what Jacob did.
When Laban and himself were compromised
That all the eanlings which were streak'd and pied
Should fall as Jacob's hire, the ewes, being rank,
Turned to the rams, and, when the work of generation
Was between these woolly breeders in the act,
the fulsome ewes, then conceiving did in eaning time
Fall parti-colour'd lambs, and those were Jacob's.
This was a way to thrive, and he was blest:
And thrift is blessing, if men steal it not.

ANTONIO   This was a venture, sir, that Jacob served for;
A thing not in his power to bring to pass,
But sway'd and fashion'd by the hand of heaven.

                Was this inserted to make interest good?
                Or is your gold and silver ewes and rams?

SHYLOCK   I cannot tell; I make it breed as fast:
                But note me, signior.

ANTONIO   Mark you this, Bassanio,
                The devil can cite Scripture for his purpose.
                An evil soul producing holy witness
                Is like a villain with a smiling cheek,
                A goodly apple rotten at the heart:
                O, what a goodly outside falsehood hath!

SHYLOCK   Three thousand ducats; 'tis a good round sum.
                Three months from twelve; then, let me see; the rate.

ANTONIO   Well, Shylock, shall we be beholding to you?

SHYLOCK   Signior Antonio, many a time and oft
                In the Rialto you have rated me
                About my moneys and my usances:
                Still have I borne it with a patient shrug,
                For sufferance is the badge of all our tribe.
                You call me misbeliever, cut-throat dog,
                And spit upon my Jewish gaberdine,
                And all for use of that which is mine own.
                Well then, it now appears you need my help:
                Go to, then; you come to me, and you say
                'Shylock, we would have moneys:' you say so;
                You, that did void your rheum upon my beard
                And foot me as you spurn a stranger cur
                Over your threshold: moneys is your suit
                What should I say to you? Should I not say
                'Hath a dog money? is it possible
                A cur can lend three thousand ducats?' Or
                Shall I bend low and in a bondman's key,
                With bated breath and whispering humbleness, Say this;
                'Fair sir, you spit on me on Wednesday last;
                You spurn'd me such a day; another time

	You call'd me dog; and for these courtesies I'll lend you thus much moneys'?
ANTONIO	I am as like to call thee so again, To spit on thee again, to spurn thee too. If thou wilt lend this money, lend it not As to thy friends; for when did friendship take A breed for barren metal of his friend? But lend it rather to thine enemy, Who, if he break, thou mayst with better face Exact the penalty.
SHYLOCK	Why, look you, how you storm! I would be friends with you and have your love, Forget the shames that you have stain'd me with, Supply your present wants and take no doit Of usance for my moneys, and you'll not hear me: This is kind I offer.
BASSANIO	This were kindness.
SHYLOCK	This kindness will I show. Go with me to a notary, seal me there Your single bond; and, in a merry sport, If you repay me not on such a day, In such a place, such sum or sums as are Express'd in the condition, let the forfeit Be nominated for an equal pound Of your fair flesh, to be cut off and taken In what part of your body pleaseth me.
ANTONIO	Content, i' faith: I'll seal to such a bond And say there is much kindness in the Jew.
BASSANIO	You shall not seal to such a bond for me: I'll rather dwell in my necessity.
ANTONIO	Why, fear not, man; I will not forfeit it: Within these two months, that's a month before

	This bond expires, I do expect return
	Of thrice three times the value of this bond.
SHYLOCK	O father Abram, what these Christians are,
	Whose own hard dealings teaches them suspect
	The thoughts of others! Pray you, tell me this;
	If he should break his day, what should I gain
	By the exaction of the forfeiture?
	A pound of man's flesh taken from a man
	Is not so estimable, profitable neither,
	As flesh of muttons, beefs, or goats. I say,
	To buy his favour, I extend this friendship:
	If he will take it, so; if not, adieu;
	And, for my love, I pray you wrong me not.
ANTONIO	Yes Shylock, I will seal unto this bond.
SHYLOCK	Then meet me forthwith at the notary's;
	Give him direction for this merry bond,
	And I will go and purse the ducats straight,
	See to my house, left in the fearful guard
	Of an unthrifty knave, and presently
	I will be with you.
ANTONIO	Hie thee, gentle Jew.

Exit SHYLOCK

	The Hebrew will turn Christian: he grows kind.
BASSANIO	I like not fair terms and a villain's mind.
ANTONIO	Come on: in this there can be no dismay;
	My ships come home a month before the day.

Exeunt

ACT II SCENE I

Belmont. A room in PORTIA'S house.

Flourish of cornets. Enter the PRINCE OF MOROCCO and his train; PORTIA, NERISSA, and others attending

MOROCCO   Mislike me not for my complexion,
The shadow'd livery of the burnish'd sun,
To whom I am a neighbour and near bred.
I tell thee, lady, I would not change this hue,
Except to steal your thoughts, my gentle queen.

PORTIA   The lottery of my destiny
Bars me the right of voluntary choosing:
But yourself, renowned prince, then stood as fair
As any comer I have look'd on yet
For my affection.

MOROCCO   Even for that I thank you:
Therefore, I pray you, lead me to the caskets
To try my fortune.

PORTIA   You must take your chance,
And either not attempt to choose at all
Or swear before you choose, if you choose wrong
Never to speak to lady afterward
In way of marriage: therefore be advised.
First, forward to the temple: after dinner
Your hazard shall be made.

MOROCCO   Good fortune then!
To make me blest or cursed'st among men.

Cornets, and exeunt

ACT II SCENE II

Venice. A street.

Enter LAUNCELOT

LAUNCELOT Certainly my conscience will serve me to run from this Jew my master. The fiend is at mine elbow and tempts me saying to me 'Launcelot Gobbo, good Launcelot, use your legs, take the start, run away. My conscience says 'No; take heed,' honest Launcelot; do not run; scorn running with thy heels.' 'Conscience,' say I, 'you counsel well;' ' Fiend,' say I, 'you counsel well:' to be ruled by my conscience, I should stay with the Jew my master, who, God bless the mark, is a kind of devil; and, to run away from the Jew, I should be ruled by the fiend, who, saving your reverence, is the devil himself. Certainly the Jew is the very devil incarnal; and, in my conscience, my conscience is but a kind of hard conscience, to offer to counsel me to stay with the Jew. The fiend gives the more friendly counsel: I will run, fiend; my heels are at your command; I will run.

Enter Old GOBBO, with a basket

LAUNCELOT [Aside] O heavens, this is my true-begotten father! who, being more than sand-blind, high-gravel blind, knows me not.

GOBBO Master young gentleman, I pray you, which is the way to master Jew's?

LAUNCELOT Do you not know me, father?

GOBBO Alack, sir, I am sand-blind; I know you not.

LAUNCELOT Nay, indeed, if you had your eyes, you might fail of the knowing me: it is a wise father that knows his

	own child. Pray you, let's have no more fooling about it, but give me your blessing: I am Launcelot, your boy that was, your son that is, your child that shall be.
GOBBO	Lord, how art thou changed! How dost thou and thy master agree? I have brought him a present. How 'gree you now?
LAUNCELOT	Well, well: but, for mine own part, as I have set up my rest to run away, so I will not rest till I have run some ground. My master's a very Jew: give him a present! give him a halter: I am famished in his service; you may tell every finger I have with my ribs. Father, I am glad you are come: give your present to one Master Bassanio, who, indeed, gives rare new liveries: if I serve not him, I will run as far as God has any ground. O rare fortune! here comes the man: to him, father; for I am a Jew, if I serve the Jew any longer.

Enter BASSANIO, with LEONARDO and other followers

LAUNCELOT	To him, father.
GOBBO	God bless your worship!
BASSANIO	Gramercy! wouldst thou aught with me?
GOBBO	Here's my son, sir, a poor boy.
LAUNCELOT	Not a poor boy, sir, but the rich Jew's man. To be brief, the very truth is that the Jew, having done me wrong, doth cause me, as my father, being, I hope, an old man, shall frutify unto you…
GOBBO	I have here a dish of doves that I would bestow upon your worship, and my suit is…
BASSANIO	One speak for both. What would you?

LAUNCELOT	Serve you, sir.
BASSANIO	I know thee well; thou hast obtain'd thy suit: Shylock thy master spoke with me this day, And hath preferr'd thee, if it be preferment To leave a rich Jew's service, to become The follower of so poor a gentleman.
LAUNCELOT	The old proverb is very well parted between my master Shylock and you, sir: you have the grace of God, sir, and he hath enough.
BASSANIO	Thou speak'st it well. Go, father, with thy son. Take leave of thy old master and inquire My lodging out. Give him a livery More guarded than his fellows': see it done.
LAUNCELOT	Father, come; I'll take my leave of the Jew in the twinkling of an eye.

Exeunt Launcelot and Old Gobbo

Enter GRATIANO

GRATIANO	Where is your master?
LEONARDO	Yonder, sir, he walks.

Exit LEONARDO

GRATIANO	Signior Bassanio!
BASSANIO	Gratiano!
GRATIANO	I have a suit to you.
BASSANIO	You have obtain'd it.
GRATIANO	You must not deny me: I must go with you to Belmont.

BASSANIO Why then you must. But hear thee, Gratiano;
Thou art too wild, too rude and bold of voice;
Parts that become thee happily enough
And in such eyes as ours appear not faults;
But where thou art not known, why, there they show
Something too liberal. Pray thee, take pain
To allay with some cold drops of modesty
Thy skipping spirit, lest through thy wild behaviour
I be misconstrued in the place I go to,
And lose my hopes.

GRATIANO Signior Bassanio, hear me:
If I do not put on a sober habit,
Talk with respect and swear but now and then,
Wear prayer-books in my pocket, look demurely,
Nay more, while grace is saying, hood mine eyes
Thus with my hat, and sigh and say 'amen,'
Use all the observance of civility,
Like one well studied in a sad ostent
To please his grandam, never trust me more.

BASSANIO Well, we shall see your bearing.

GRATIANO Nay, but I bar to-night: you shall not gauge me
By what we do to-night.

BASSANIO No, that were pity:
I would entreat you rather to put on
Your boldest suit of mirth, for we have friends
That purpose merriment. But fare you well:
I have some business.

GRATIANO And I must to Lorenzo and the rest:
But we will visit you at supper-time.

Exeunt

ACT II SCENE III

The same. A room in SHYLOCK'S house.

Enter JESSICA and LAUNCELOT

JESSICA   I am sorry thou wilt leave my father so:
Our house is hell, and thou, a merry devil,
Didst rob it of some taste of tediousness.
But fare thee well, there is a ducat for thee:
And, Launcelot, soon at supper shalt thou see
Lorenzo, who is thy new master's guest:
Give him this letter; do it secretly;
And so farewell: I would not have my father
See me in talk with thee.

LAUNCELOT   Adieu! tears exhibit my tongue. Most beautiful
pagan, most sweet Jew! if a Christian did not play
the knave and get thee, I am much deceived. But,
adieu: these foolish drops do something drown my
manly spirit: adieu.

JESSICA   Farewell, good Launcelot.

Exit Launcelot

Alack, what heinous sin is it in me
To be ashamed to be my father's child!
But though I am a daughter to his blood,
I am not to his manners. O Lorenzo,
If thou keep promise, I shall end this strife,
Become a Christian and thy loving wife.

Exit

ACT II SCENE IV

The same. A street.

Enter GRATIANO, LORENZO, SALARINO, and SALANIO

LORENZO	Nay, we will slink away in supper-time, Disguise us at my lodging and return, All in an hour.
GRATIANO	We have not made good preparation.
SALARINO	We have not spoke us yet of torchbearers.
SALANIO	'Tis vile, unless it may be quaintly order'd, And better in my mind not undertook.
LORENZO	'Tis now but four o'clock: we have two hours To furnish us.

Enter LAUNCELOT, with a letter

	Friend Launcelot, what's the news?
LAUNCELOT	An it shall please you to break up this, it shall seem to signify.
LORENZO	I know the hand: in faith, 'tis a fair hand; And whiter than the paper it writ on Is the fair hand that writ.
GRATIANO	Love-news, in faith.
LAUNCELOT	By your leave, sir.
LORENZO	Whither goest thou?
LAUNCELOT	Marry, sir, to bid my old master the Jew To sup to-night with my new master the Christian.

LORENZO Hold here, take this: tell gentle Jessica
I will not fail her; speak it privately.
Go, gentlemen,

Exit Launcelot

Will you prepare you for this masque tonight?
I am provided of a torch-bearer.

SALANIO Ay, marry, I'll be gone about it straight.

SALARINO And so will I.

LORENZO Meet me and Gratiano
At Gratiano's lodging some hour hence.

SALARINO 'Tis good we do so.

Exeunt SALARINO and SALANIO

GRATIANO Was not that letter from fair Jessica?

LORENZO I must needs tell thee all. She hath directed
How I shall take her from her father's house,
What gold and jewels she is furnish'd with,
What page's suit she hath in readiness.
If e'er the Jew her father come to heaven,
It will be for his gentle daughter's sake:
And never dare misfortune cross her foot,
Unless she do it under this excuse,
That she is issue to a faithless Jew.
Come, go with me; peruse this as thou goest:
Fair Jessica shall be my torch-bearer.

Exeunt

ACT II SCENE V

The same. Before SHYLOCK'S house.

Enter SHYLOCK and LAUNCELOT

SHYLOCK Well, thou shalt see, thy eyes shall be thy judge,
The difference of old Shylock and Bassanio:-
What, Jessica!-thou shalt not gormandise,
As thou hast done with me:-What, Jessica!-
And sleep and snore, and rend apparel out;-
Why, Jessica, I say!

Enter Jessica

JESSICA Call you? what is your will?

SHYLOCK I am bid forth to supper, Jessica:
There are my keys. But wherefore should I go?
I am not bid for love; they flatter me:
But yet I'll go in hate, to feed upon
The prodigal Christian. Jessica, my girl,
Look to my house. I am right loath to go:
There is some ill a-brewing towards my rest,
For I did dream of money-bags to-night.

LAUNCELOT I beseech you, sir, go: my young master doth expect
your reproach.

SHYLOCK So do I his.

LAUNCELOT An they have conspired together, I will not say you
shall see a masque; but if you do, then it was not
for nothing that my nose fell a-bleeding on
Black-Monday last at six o'clock i' the morning.

SHYLOCK What, are there masques? Hear you me, Jessica:
Lock up my doors; and when you hear the drum
And the vile squealing of the wry-neck'd fife,

	Clamber not you up to the casements then,
	Nor thrust your head into the public street
	To gaze on Christian fools with varnish'd faces.
	I have no mind of feasting forth to-night:
	But I will go. Go you before me, sirrah;
	Say I will come.
LAUNCELOT	I will go before, sir. Mistress, look out at window, for all this, There will come a Christian boy, will be worth a Jewess' eye.

Exit

SHYLOCK	Well, Jessica, go in;
	Perhaps I will return immediately:
	Do as I bid you; shut doors after you:
	Fast bind, fast find;
	A proverb never stale in thrifty mind.

Exit

JESSICA	Farewell; and if my fortune be not crost,
	I have a father, you a daughter, lost.

Exit

ACT II SCENE VI

The same.

Enter GRATIANO and SALARINO, masqued

GRATIANO This is the pent-house under which Lorenzo
Desired us to make stand.

SALARINO Here comes Lorenzo.

Enter LORENZO

LORENZO Sweet friends, approach;
Here dwells my father Jew. Ho! who's within?

Enter JESSICA, above, in boy's clothes

JESSICA Who are you? Tell me, for more certainty,
Albeit I'll swear that I do know your tongue.

LORENZO Lorenzo, and thy love.

JESSICA Lorenzo, certain, and my love indeed.
Here, catch this casket; it is worth the pains.
I am glad 'tis night, you do not look on me,
For Cupid himself would blush
To see me thus transformed to a boy.

LORENZO Descend, for you must be my torchbearer.

JESSICA I will make fast the doors, and gild myself
With some more ducats, and be with you straight.

Exit above

GRATIANO Now, by my hood, a Gentile and no Jew.

LORENZO Beshrew me but I love her heartily.

Enter JESSICA, below

What, art thou come? On, gentlemen; away!
Our masquing mates by this time for us stay.

Exeunt

ACT II SCENE VII

Belmont. A room in PORTIA'S house.

Flourish of cornets. Enter PORTIA, with the PRINCE OF MOROCCO, and their trains

PORTIA
Go draw aside the curtains and discover
The several caskets to this noble prince.
Now make your choice.

MOROCCO
The first, of gold, who this inscription bears,
'Who chooseth me shall gain what many men desire;'
The second, silver, which this promise carries,
'Who chooseth me shall get as much as he deserves;'
This third, dull lead, with warning all as blunt,
'Who chooseth me must give and hazard all he hath.'
How shall I know if I do choose the right?

PORTIA
The one of them contains my picture, prince:
If you choose that, then I am yours withal.

MOROCCO
Some god direct my judgment! Let me see;
I will survey the inscriptions back again.
What says this leaden casket?
'Who chooseth me must give and hazard all he hath.'
Must give: for what? for lead? hazard for lead?
What says the silver with her virgin hue?
'Who chooseth me shall get as much as he deserves.'
As much as I deserve! Why, that's the lady:
I do in birth deserve her, and in fortunes,
In graces and in qualities of breeding;
But more than these, in love I do deserve.
Let's see once more this saying graved in gold
'Who chooseth me shall gain what many men desire.'
Why, that's the lady; all the world desires her;
From the four corners of the earth they come,
To kiss this shrine, this mortal-breathing saint:
One of these three contains her heavenly picture.
Is't like that lead contains her?

	Or shall I think in silver she's immured,
	O sinful thought! Never so rich a gem
	Was set in worse than gold. Deliver me the key:
	Here do I choose, and thrive I as I may!
PORTIA	There, take it, prince; and if my form lie there,
	Then I am yours.

He unlocks the golden casket

MOROCCO	O hell! what have we here?
	A carrion Death, within whose empty eye
	There is a written scroll! I'll read the writing.
Reads	All that glitters is not gold;
	Often have you heard that told:
	Many a man his life hath sold
	But my outside to behold:
	Gilded tombs do worms enfold.
	Had you been as wise as bold,
	Young in limbs, in judgment old,
	Your answer had not been inscroll'd:
	Fare you well; your suit is cold.
	Cold, indeed; and labour lost:
	Then, farewell, heat, and welcome, frost!
	Portia, adieu. I have too grieved a heart
	To take a tedious leave: thus losers part.

Exit with his train. Flourish of cornets

PORTIA	A gentle riddance. Draw the curtains, go.
	Let all of his complexion choose me so.

Exeunt

ACT II SCENE VIII

Venice. A street.

Enter SALARINO and SALANIO

SALARINO Why, man, I saw Bassanio under sail:
With him is Gratiano gone along;
And in their ship I am sure Lorenzo is not.

SALANIO The villain Jew with outcries raised the duke,
Who went with him to search Bassanio's ship.

SALARINO He came too late, the ship was under sail:
Besides, Antonio certified the duke
They were not with Bassanio in his ship.

SALANIO I never heard a passion so confused,
So strange, outrageous, and so variable,
As the dog Jew did utter in the streets:
'My daughter! O my ducats! O my daughter!
Fled with a Christian! O my Christian ducats!
Justice! the law! my ducats, and my daughter!
A sealed bag, two sealed bags of ducats,
Of double ducats, stolen from me by my daughter!
And jewels, two stones, two rich and precious stones,
Stolen by my daughter! Justice! find the girl;
She hath the stones upon her, and the ducats.'
Let good Antonio look he keep his day,
Or he shall pay for this.

SALARINO Marry, well remember'd.
I reason'd with a Frenchman yesterday,
Who told me, in the narrow seas that part
The French and English, there miscarried
A vessel of our country richly fraught:
I thought upon Antonio when he told me;
And wish'd in silence that it were not his.

SALANIO You were best to tell Antonio what you hear;
Yet do not suddenly, for it may grieve him.

SALARINO A kinder gentleman treads not the earth.

SALANIO I pray thee, let us go and find him out
And quicken his embraced heaviness
With some delight or other.

Exeunt

ACT II SCENE IX

Belmont. A room in PORTIA'S house.

Enter NERISSA with a Servant

NERISSA   Quick, quick, I pray thee; draw the curtain straight:
The Prince of Arragon hath ta'en his oath,
And comes to his election presently.

Flourish of cornets. Enter the PRINCE OF ARRAGON, PORTIA, and their trains

PORTIA   Behold, there stand the caskets, noble prince:
If you choose that wherein I am contain'd,
Straight shall our nuptial rites be solemnized:
But if you fail, without more speech, my lord,
You must be gone from hence immediately.

ARRAGON   I am enjoin'd by oath to observe three things:
First, never to unfold to any one
Which casket 'twas I chose; next, if I fail
Of the right casket, never in my life
To woo a maid in way of marriage: Lastly,
If I do fail in fortune of my choice,
Immediately to leave you and be gone.

PORTIA   To these injunctions every one doth swear
That comes to hazard for my worthless self.

ARRAGON   And so have I address'd me. Fortune now
To my heart's hope! Gold; silver; and base lead.
'Who chooseth me must give and hazard all he hath.'
You shall look fairer, ere I give or hazard.
What says the golden chest? ha! let me see:
'Who chooseth me shall gain what many men desire.'
What many men desire! that 'many' may be meant
By the fool multitude, that choose by show,
Not learning more than the fond eye doth teach;
I will not choose what many men desire,

Because I will not jump with common spirits
And rank me with the barbarous multitudes.
Why, then to thee, thou silver treasure-house;
'Who chooseth me shall get as much as he deserves:'
And well said too; for who shall go about
To cozen fortune and be honourable
Without the stamp of merit? Well, but to my choice:
'Who chooseth me shall get as much as he deserves.'
I will assume desert. Give me a key for this,
And instantly unlock my fortunes here.

He opens the silver casket

PORTIA   Too long a pause for that which you find there.

ARRAGON   What's here? the portrait of a blinking idiot.
Did I deserve no more than a fool's head?
Is that my prize? are my deserts no better?

PORTIA   To offend, and judge, are distinct offices
And of opposed natures.

ARRAGON   What is here?

Reads   The fire seven times tried this:
Seven times tried that judgment is,
That did never choose amiss.
Some there be that shadows kiss;
Such have but a shadow's bliss:
There be fools alive, I wis,
Silver'd o'er; and so was this.
Take what wife you will to bed,
I will ever be your head:
So be gone: you are sped.
Still more fool I shall appear
By the time I linger here
With one fool's head I came to woo,
But I go away with two.
Sweet, adieu. I'll keep my oath,
Patiently to bear my wroth.

Exeunt Arragon and train

PORTIA Thus hath the candle singed the moth.
O, these deliberate fools! when they do choose,
They have the wisdom by their wit to lose.

Enter a Servant

Servant Madam, there is alighted at your gate
A young Venetian, one that comes before
To signify the approaching of his lord;
From whom he bringeth sensible regreets,
To wit, besides commends and courteous breath,
Gifts of rich value. Yet I have not seen
So likely an ambassador of love:
A day in April never came so sweet,
To show how costly summer was at hand,
As this fore-spurrer comes before his lord.

PORTIA No more, I pray thee: I am half afeard
Thou wilt say anon he is some kin to thee,
Thou spend'st such high-day wit in praising him.
Come, come, Nerissa; for I long to see
Quick Cupid's post that comes so mannerly.

NERISSA Bassanio, lord Love, if thy will it be!

Exeunt

ACT III SCENE I

Venice. A street.

Enter SALANIO and SALARINO

SALANIO Now, what news on the Rialto?

SALARINO Why, yet it lives there uncheck'd that Antonio hath a ship of rich lading wrecked on the narrow seas.

SALANIO It is true that the good Antonio, the honest Antonio, hath lost a ship.

SALARINO I would it might prove the end of his losses.

SALANIO Let me say 'amen' betimes, lest the devil cross my prayer, for here he comes in the likeness of a Jew.

Enter SHYLOCK

How now, Shylock! what news among the merchants?

SHYLOCK You know, none so well, none so well as you, of my daughter's flight.

SALARINO That's certain: I, for my part, knew the tailor that made the wings she flew withal.

SALANIO And Shylock, for his own part, knew the bird was fledged; and then it is the complexion of them all to leave the dam.

SHYLOCK She is damned for it.

SALANIO That's certain, if the devil may be her judge.

SHYLOCK My own flesh and blood to rebel!

SALANIO Out upon it, old carrion! rebels it at these years?

SHYLOCK I say, my daughter is my flesh and blood.

SALARINO There is more difference between thy flesh and hers than between jet and ivory; more between your bloods than there is between red wine and rhenish. But tell us, do you hear whether Antonio have had any loss at sea or no?

SHYLOCK There I have another bad match: a bankrupt, a prodigal, who dare scarce show his head on the Rialto; a beggar, that was used to come so smug upon the mart; let him look to his bond: he was wont to call me usurer; let him look to his bond: he was wont to lend money for a Christian courtesy; let him look to his bond.

SALARINO Why, I am sure, if he forfeit, thou wilt not take his flesh: what's that good for?

SHYLOCK To bait fish withal: if it will feed nothing else, it will feed my revenge. He hath disgraced me, and hindered me half a million; laughed at my losses, mocked at my gains, scorned my nation, thwarted my bargains, cooled my friends, heated mine enemies; and what's his reason? I am a Jew. Hath not a Jew eyes? hath not a Jew hands, organs, dimensions, senses, affections, passions? fed with the same food, hurt with the same weapons, subject to the same diseases, healed by the same means, warmed and cooled by the same winter and summer, as a Christian is? If you prick us, do we not bleed? if you tickle us, do we not laugh? if you poison us, do we not die? and if you wrong us, shall we not revenge? If we are like you in the rest, we will resemble you in that. If a Jew wrong a Christian, what is his humility? Revenge. If a Christian wrong a Jew, what should his sufferance be by Christian example? Why, revenge. The villany you

	teach me, I will execute, and it shall go hard but I will better the instruction.

Enter a Servant

Servant	Gentlemen, my master Antonio is at his house and desires to speak with you both.
SALARINO	We have been up and down to seek him.

Enter TUBAL

SALANIO	Here comes another of the tribe: a third cannot be matched, unless the devil himself turn Jew.

Exeunt SALANIO, SALARINO, and Servant

SHYLOCK	How now, Tubal! what news from Genoa? hast thou found my daughter?
TUBAL	I often came where I did hear of her, but cannot find her.
SHYLOCK	Why, there, there, there, there! a diamond gone, cost me two thousand ducats in Frankfort! The curse never fell upon our nation till now; I never felt it till now: two thousand ducats in that; and other precious, precious jewels. I would my daughter were dead at my foot, and the jewels in her ear! would she were hearsed at my foot, and the ducats in her coffin! No news of them? Why, so: and I know not what's spent in the search: why, thou loss upon loss! the thief gone with so much, and so much to find the thief; and no satisfaction, no revenge: nor no in luck stirring but what lights on my shoulders; no sighs but of my breathing; no tears but of my shedding.
TUBAL	Yes, other men have ill luck too: Antonio, as I heard in Genoa,-

SHYLOCK	What, what, what? ill luck, ill luck?
TUBAL	Hath an argosy cast away, coming from Tripolis.
SHYLOCK	I thank God, I thank God. Is't true, is't true?
TUBAL	I spoke with some of the sailors that escaped the wreck.
SHYLOCK	I thank thee, good Tubal: good news, good news! ha, ha! where? in Genoa?
TUBAL	Your daughter spent in Genoa, as I heard, in one night fourscore ducats.
SHYLOCK	Thou stickest a dagger in me: I shall never see my gold again: fourscore ducats at a sitting! fourscore ducats!
TUBAL	There came divers of Antonio's creditors in my company to Venice, that swear he cannot choose but break.
SHYLOCK	I am very glad of it: I'll plague him; I'll torture him: I am glad of it.
TUBAL	One of them showed me a ring that he had of your daughter for a monkey.
SHYLOCK	Out upon her! Thou torturest me, Tubal: it was my turquoise; I had it of Leah when I was a bachelor: I would not have given it for a wilderness of monkeys.
TUBAL	But Antonio is certainly undone.
SHYLOCK	Nay, that's true, that's very true. Go, Tubal, fee me an officer; bespeak him a fortnight before. I will have the heart of him, if he forfeit; for, were he out of Venice, I can make what merchandise I will. Go, go, Tubal, and meet me at our synagogue; go, good Tubal; at our synagogue, Tubal.

Exeunt

ACT III SCENE II

Belmont. A room in PORTIA'S house.

Enter BASSANIO, PORTIA, GRATIANO, NERISSA, and Attendants

PORTIA I pray you, tarry: pause a day or two
Before you hazard; for, in choosing wrong,
I lose your company: therefore forbear awhile.
There's something tells me, but it is not love,
I would not lose you;
But lest you should not understand me well,
I would detain you here some month or two
Before you venture for me. I could teach you
How to choose right, but I am then forsworn;
So will I never be: so may you miss me;
But if you do, you'll make me wish a sin,
That I had been forsworn.

BASSANIO Let me choose
For as I am, I live upon the rack.

PORTIA Upon the rack, Bassanio! then confess
What treason there is mingled with your love.

BASSANIO None but that ugly treason of mistrust,
Which makes me fear the enjoying of my love:
There may as well be amity and life
'Tween snow and fire, as treason and my love.

PORTIA Ay, but I fear you speak upon the rack,
Where men enforced do speak anything.

BASSANIO Promise me life, and I'll confess the truth.

PORTIA Well then, confess and live.

BASSANIO 'Confess' and 'love'
Had been the very sum of my confession:
O happy torment, when my torturer

	Doth teach me answers for deliverance!
	But let me to my fortune and the caskets.
PORTIA	Away, then! I am lock'd in one of them:
	If you do love me, you will find me out.

Music, whilst BASSANIO comments on the caskets to himself

SONG	Tell me where is fancy bred,
	Or in the heart, or in the head?
	How begot, how nourished?
	Reply, reply.
	It is engender'd in the eyes,
	With gazing fed; and fancy dies
	In the cradle where it lies.
	Let us all ring fancy's knell
	I'll begin it,--Ding, dong, bell.
ALL	Ding, dong, bell.
BASSANIO	So may the outward shows be least themselves:
	The world is still deceived with ornament.
	Look on beauty,
	And you shall see 'tis purchased by the weight;
	Which therein works a miracle in nature,
	Making them lightest that wear most of it:
	Thus ornament is but the guiled shore
	To a most dangerous sea; the beauteous scarf
	Veiling an Indian beauty; in a word,
	The seeming truth which cunning times put on
	To entrap the wisest. Therefore, thou gaudy gold,
	Hard food for Midas, I will none of thee;
	Nor none of thee, thou pale and common drudge
	'Tween man and man: but thou, thou meagre lead,
	Which rather threatenest than dost promise aught,
	Thy paleness moves me more than eloquence;
	And here choose I; joy be the consequence!
	What find I here?

Opening the leaden casket

Fair Portia's counterfeit! What demi-god
Hath come so near creation? Move these eyes?
Or whether, riding on the balls of mine,
Seem they in motion? Here are sever'd lips,
Parted with sugar breath: so sweet a bar
Should sunder such sweet friends. Yet look, how far
The substance of my praise doth wrong this shadow
In underprizing it, so far this shadow
Doth limp behind the substance. Here's the scroll,
The continent and summary of my fortune.

Reads

You that choose not by the view,
Chance as fair and choose as true!
Since this fortune falls to you,
Be content and seek no new,
If you be well pleased with this
And hold your fortune for your bliss,
Turn you where your lady is
And claim her with a loving kiss.
A gentle scroll. Fair lady, by your leave;
I come by note, to give and to receive.
Like one of two contending in a prize,
That thinks he hath done well in people's eyes,
Hearing applause and universal shout,
Giddy in spirit, still gazing in a doubt
Whether these pearls of praise be his or no;
So, thrice fair lady, stand I, even so;
As doubtful whether what I see be true,
Until confirm'd, sign'd, ratified by you.

PORTIA

You see me, Lord Bassanio, where I stand,
Such as I am: though for myself alone
I would not be ambitious in my wish,
To wish myself much better; yet, for you
I would be trebled twenty times myself;
A thousand times more fair, ten thousand times more rich;
That only to stand high in your account,
I might in virtue, beauties, livings, friends,
Exceed account; but the full sum of me

	Is sum of something, which, to term in gross,
	Is an unlesson'd girl, unschool'd, unpractised;
	Happy in this, she is not yet so old
	But she may learn; happier than this,
	She is not bred so dull but she can learn;
	Happiest of all is that her gentle spirit
	Commits itself to yours to be directed,
	As from her lord, her governor, her king.
	Myself and what is mine to you and yours
	Is now converted: but now I was the lord
	Of this fair mansion, master of my servants,
	Queen o'er myself: and even now, but now,
	This house, these servants and this same myself
	Are yours, my lord: I give them with this ring;
	Which when you part from, lose, or give away,
	Let it presage the ruin of your love
	And be my vantage to exclaim on you.
BASSANIO	Madam, you have bereft me of all words,
	But when this ring
	Parts from this finger, then parts life from hence:
	O, then be bold to say Bassanio's dead!
GRATIANO	My lord Bassanio and my gentle lady,
	I wish you all the joy that you can wish;
	For I am sure you can wish none from me:
	And when your honours mean to solemnize
	The bargain of your faith, I do beseech you,
	Even at that time I may be married too.
BASSANIO	With all my heart, so thou canst get a wife.
GRATIANO	I thank your lordship, you have got me one.
	My eyes, my lord, can look as swift as yours:
	You saw the mistress, I beheld the maid;
	Your fortune stood upon the casket there,
	And so did mine too, as the matter falls;
	I got a promise of this fair one here
	To have her love, provided that your fortune
	Achieved her mistress.

PORTIA Is this true, Nerissa?

NERISSA Madam, it is, so you stand pleased withal.

BASSANIO And do you, Gratiano, mean good faith?

GRATIANO Yes, faith, my lord.

BASSANIO Our feast shall be much honour'd in your marriage.

GRATIANO But who comes here? Lorenzo and his infidel? What,
and my old Venetian friend Salerio?

Enter LORENZO, JESSICA, and SALERIO, a Messenger from Venice

BASSANIO Lorenzo and Salerio, welcome hither;
By your leave,
I bid my very friends and countrymen,
Sweet Portia, welcome.

PORTIA So do I, my lord:
They are entirely welcome.

LORENZO I thank your honour. For my part, my lord,
My purpose was not to have seen you here;
But meeting with Salerio by the way,
He did entreat me, past all saying nay,
To come with him along.

SALERIO I did, my lord; and I have reason for it.
Signior Antonio commends him to you.

Gives Bassanio a letter

BASSANIO Ere I ope his letter,
I pray you, tell me how my good friend doth.

SALERIO   Not sick, my lord, unless it be in mind;
Nor well, unless in mind: his letter there
Will show you his estate.

GRATIANO   Nerissa, cheer yon stranger; bid her welcome.
Your hand, Salerio: what's the news from Venice?
How doth that royal merchant, good Antonio?
I know he will be glad of our success;
We are the Jasons, we have won the fleece.

SALERIO   I would you had won the fleece that he hath lost.

PORTIA   There are some shrewd contents in yon same paper,
That steals the colour from Bassanio's cheek:
Some dear friend dead; else nothing in the world
Could turn so much the constitution
Of any constant man. What, worse and worse!
With leave, Bassanio: I am half yourself,
And I must freely have the half of anything
That this same paper brings you.

BASSANIO   O sweet Portia,
Here are a few of the unpleasant'st words
That ever blotted paper! Gentle lady,
When I did first impart my love to you,
I freely told you, all the wealth I had
Ran in my veins, I was a gentleman;
And then I told you true: and yet, dear lady,
Rating myself at nothing, you shall see
How much I was a braggart. For, indeed,
I have engaged my friend to his mere enemy,
To feed my means. Here is a letter, lady;
The paper as the body of my friend,
And every word in it a gaping wound,
Issuing life-blood. But is it true, Salerio?
Have all his ventures fail'd? What, not one hit?

SALERIO   Not one, my lord.
Besides, it should appear, that if he had
The present money to discharge the Jew,

	He would not take it. Never did I know
	A creature, that did bear the shape of man,
	So keen and greedy to confound a man:
	He plies the duke at morning and at night,
	And doth impeach the freedom of the state,
	If they deny him justice: twenty merchants,
	The duke himself, and the magnificoes
	Of greatest port, have all persuaded with him;
	But none can drive him from the envious plea
	Of forfeiture, of justice and his bond.
JESSICA	When I was with him I have heard him swear
	That he would rather have Antonio's flesh
	Than twenty times the value of the sum
	That he did owe him: and I know, my lord,
	If law, authority and power deny not,
	It will go hard with poor Antonio.
PORTIA	Is it your dear friend that is thus in trouble?
BASSANIO	The dearest friend to me, the kindest man,
	The best-condition'd and unwearied spirit
	In doing courtesies, and one in whom
	The ancient Roman honour more appears
	Than any that draws breath in Italy.
PORTIA	What sum owes he the Jew?
BASSANIO	For me three thousand ducats.
PORTIA	What, no more?
	Pay him six thousand, and deface the bond;
	Double six thousand, and then treble that,
	Before a friend of this description
	Shall lose a hair through Bassanio's fault.
	First go with me to church and call me wife,
	And then away to Venice to your friend;
	For never shall you lie by Portia's side
	With an unquiet soul. You shall have gold
	To pay the petty debt twenty times over:

	When it is paid, bring your true friend along.
	My maid Nerissa and myself meantime
	Will live as maids and widows.
	But let me hear the letter of your friend.

BASSANIO [Reads] Sweet Bassanio, my ships have all miscarried, my creditors grow cruel, my estate is very low, my bond to the Jew is forfeit; and since in paying it, it is impossible I should live, all debts are cleared between you and I, if I might but see you at my death. Notwithstanding, use your pleasure: if your love do not persuade you to come, let not my letter.

PORTIA O love, dispatch all business, and be gone!

BASSANIO Since I have your good leave to go away, I will make haste.

Exeunt

ACT III SCENE III

Venice. A street.

Enter SHYLOCK, SALARINO and ANTONIO

ANTONIO   Hear me yet, good Shylock.

SHYLOCK   I'll have my bond; speak not against my bond:
I have sworn an oath that I will have my bond.
Thou call'dst me dog before thou hadst a cause;
But, since I am a dog, beware my fangs:
The duke shall grant me justice.

ANTONIO   I pray thee, hear me speak.

SHYLOCK   I'll have my bond; I will not hear thee speak:
I'll have my bond; and therefore speak no more.
I'll not be made a soft and dull-eyed fool,
To shake the head, relent, and sigh, and yield
To Christian intercessors. Follow not;
I'll have no speaking: I will have my bond.

Exit

SALARINO   It is the most impenetrable cur
That ever kept with men.

ANTONIO   Let him alone:
I'll follow him no more with bootless prayers.
He seeks my life; his reason well I know:
I oft deliver'd from his forfeitures
Many that have at times made moan to me;
Therefore he hates me.

SALARINO   I am sure the duke
Will never grant this forfeiture to hold.

ANTONIO   The duke cannot deny the course of law:
For the commodity that strangers have

With us in Venice, if it be denied,
Will much impeach the justice of his state;
Since that the trade and profit of the city
Consisteth of all nations. Therefore, go:
These griefs and losses have so bated me,
That I shall hardly spare a pound of flesh
To-morrow to my bloody creditor.

Exeunt

ACT III SCENE IV

Belmont. A room in PORTIA'S house.

Enter PORTIA, NERISSA, LORENZO, JESSICA, and BALTHASAR

LORENZO Madam, although I speak it in your presence,
You have a noble and a true conceit
Of godlike amity; which appears most strongly
In bearing thus the absence of your lord.
But if you knew to whom you show this honour,
How true a gentleman you send relief,
How dear a lover of my lord your husband,
I know you would be prouder of the work
Than customary bounty can enforce you.

PORTIA I never did repent for doing good,
Nor shall not now: for this Antonio,
Being the bosom lover of my lord,
Must needs be like my lord. If it be so,
How little is the cost I have bestow'd
In purchasing the semblance of my soul
From out the state of hellish misery!
This comes too near the praising of myself;
Therefore no more of it: for mine own part,
I have toward heaven breathed a secret vow
To live in prayer and contemplation,
Only attended by Nerissa here,
Until her husband and my lord's return:
There is a monastery two miles off;
And there will we abide.

Exeunt JESSICA and LORENZO

PORTIA Now, Balthasar, take this same letter,
In speed to Padua: see thou render this
Into my cousin's hand, Doctor Bellario;
And, look, what notes and garments he doth give thee,
Bring them, I pray thee, to Venice.

	Waste no time in words,
	But get thee gone: I shall be there before thee.
BALTHASAR	Madam, I go with all convenient speed.

Exit

PORTIA	Come on, Nerissa; I have work in hand
	That you yet know not of: we'll see our husbands
	Before they think of us.
NERISSA	Shall they see us?
PORTIA	They shall, Nerissa; but in such a habit,
	That they shall think we are accomplished
	With that we lack. I'll hold thee any wager,
	When we are both accoutred like young men,
	I'll prove the prettier fellow of the two.
NERISSA	Why, shall we turn to men?
PORTIA	Fie, what a question's that,
	If thou wert near a lewd interpreter!
	But come, I'll tell thee all my whole device
	When I am in my coach, which stays for us.

Exeunt

ACT IV SCENE I

Venice. A court of justice.

Enter the DUKE, the Magnificoes, ANTONIO, BASSANIO, GRATIANO, SALERIO, and others

DUKE   What, is Antonio here?

ANTONIO   Ready, so please your grace.

DUKE   I am sorry for thee: thou art come to answer
A stony adversary, an inhuman wretch
uncapable of pity, void and empty
From any dram of mercy.

ANTONIO   I have heard
Your grace hath ta'en great pains to qualify
His rigorous course; but since he stands obdurate
And that no lawful means can carry me
Out of his envy's reach, I do oppose
My patience to his fury, and am arm'd
To suffer, with a quietness of spirit,
The very tyranny and rage of his.

Enter SHYLOCK

DUKE   Shylock, the world thinks, and I think so too,
That thou but lead'st this fashion of thy malice
To the last hour of act; and then 'tis thought
Thou'lt show thy mercy and remorse more strange
Than is thy strange apparent cruelty;
And where thou now exact'st the penalty,
Which is a pound of this poor merchant's flesh,
Thou wilt not only loose the forfeiture,
But, touch'd with human gentleness and love,
Forgive a moiety of the principal;
Glancing an eye of pity on his losses,
That have of late so huddled on his back.
We all expect a gentle answer, Jew.

SHYLOCK I have possess'd your grace of what I purpose;
And by our holy Sabbath have I sworn
To have the due and forfeit of my bond:
If you deny it, let the danger light
Upon your charter and your city's freedom.
You'll ask me, why I rather choose to have
A weight of carrion flesh than to receive
Three thousand ducats: I'll not answer that:
But, say, it is my humour: is it answer'd?
What if my house be troubled with a rat
And I be pleased to give ten thousand ducats
To have it baned? What, are you answer'd yet?
Some men there are love not a gaping pig;
As there is no firm reason to be render'd,
Why he cannot abide a gaping pig;
So can I give no reason, nor I will not,
More than a lodged hate and a certain loathing
I bear Antonio, that I follow thus
A losing suit against him. Are you answer'd?

BASSANIO This is no answer, thou unfeeling man,
To excuse the current of thy cruelty.

SHYLOCK I am not bound to please thee with my answers.

BASSANIO Do all men kill the things they do not love?

SHYLOCK Hates any man the thing he would not kill?

BASSANIO Every offence is not a hate at first.

SHYLOCK What, wouldst thou have a serpent sting thee twice?

ANTONIO I pray you, think you question with the Jew:
You may as well go stand upon the beach
And bid the main flood bate his usual height;
You may as well do anything most hard,
As seek to soften that--than which what's harder?--
His Jewish heart: therefore, I do beseech you,
Make no more offers, use no farther means,

| | But with all brief and plain conveniency |
| | Let me have judgment and the Jew his will. |

BASSANIO   For thy three thousand ducats here is six.

SHYLOCK   What judgment shall I dread, doing
                   Were in six parts and every part a ducat,
                   I would not draw them; I would have my bond.

DUKE   How shalt thou hope for mercy, rendering none?

SHYLOCK   What judgment shall I dread, doing no wrong?
                   The pound of flesh, which I demand of him,
                   Is dearly bought; 'tis mine and I will have it.
                   If you deny me, fie upon your law!
                   There is no force in the decrees of Venice.
                   I stand for judgment: answer; shall I have it?

DUKE   Upon my power I may dismiss this court,
                   Unless Bellario, a learned doctor,
                   Whom I have sent for to determine this,
                   Come here to-day.

SALERIO   My lord, here stays without
                   A messenger with letters from the doctor,
                   New come from Padua.

DUKE   Bring us the letter; call the messenger.

BASSANIO   Good cheer, Antonio! What, man, courage yet!
                   The Jew shall have my flesh, blood, bones and all,
                   Ere thou shalt lose for me one drop of blood.

ANTONIO   I am a tainted wether of the flock,
                   Meetest for death: the weakest kind of fruit
                   Drops earliest to the ground; and so let me
                   You cannot better be employ'd, Bassanio,
                   Than to live still and write mine epitaph.

Enter NERISSA, dressed like a lawyer's clerk

DUKE Came you from Padua, from Bellario?

NERISSA From both, my lord. Bellario greets your grace.

Presenting a letter

BASSANIO Why dost thou whet thy knife so earnestly?

SHYLOCK To cut the forfeiture from that bankrupt there.

GRATIANO Not on thy sole, but on thy soul, harsh Jew,
Thou makest thy knife keen; but no metal can,
No, not the hangman's axe, bear half the keenness
Of thy sharp envy. Can no prayers pierce thee?

SHYLOCK No, none that thou hast wit enough to make.

GRATIANO O, be thou damn'd, inexecrable dog!
And for thy life let justice be accused.
Thou almost makest me waver in my faith
To hold opinion with Pythagoras,
That souls of animals infuse themselves
Into the trunks of men: thy currish spirit
Govern'd a wolf, who, hang'd for human slaughter,
Even from the gallows did his fell soul fleet,
And, whilst thou lay'st in thy unhallow'd dam,
Infused itself in thee; for thy desires
Are wolvish, bloody, starved and ravenous.

SHYLOCK Till thou canst rail the seal from off my bond,
Thou but offend'st thy lungs to speak so loud:
Repair thy wit, good youth, or it will fall
To cureless ruin. I stand here for law.

DUKE This letter from Bellario doth commend
A young and learned doctor to our court.
Where is he?

NERISSA	He attendeth here hard by, To know your answer, whether you'll admit him.
DUKE	With all my heart.

Enter PORTIA, dressed like a doctor of laws

	You are welcome: take your place. Are you acquainted with the difference That holds this present question in the court?
PORTIA	I am informed thoroughly of the cause. Which is the merchant here, and which the Jew?
DUKE	Antonio and old Shylock, both stand forth.
PORTIA	Is your name Shylock?
SHYLOCK	Shylock is my name.
PORTIA	Of a strange nature is the suit you follow; Yet in such rule that the Venetian law Cannot impugn you as you do proceed. You stand within his danger, do you not?
ANTONIO	Ay, so he says.
PORTIA	Do you confess the bond?
ANTONIO	I do.
PORTIA	Then must the Jew be merciful.
SHYLOCK	On what compulsion must I? tell me that.
PORTIA	The quality of mercy is not strain'd, It droppeth as the gentle rain from heaven Upon the place beneath: it is twice blest; It blesseth him that gives and him that takes: 'Tis mightiest in the mightiest: it becomes

The throned monarch better than his crown;
His sceptre shows the force of temporal power,
The attribute to awe and majesty,
Wherein doth sit the dread and fear of kings;
But mercy is above this sceptred sway;
It is enthroned in the hearts of kings,
It is an attribute to God himself;
And earthly power doth then show likest God's
When mercy seasons justice. Therefore, Jew,
Though justice be thy plea, consider this,
That, in the course of justice, none of us
Should see salvation: we do pray for mercy;
And that same prayer doth teach us all to render
The deeds of mercy. I have spoke thus much
To mitigate the justice of thy plea;
Which if thou follow, this strict court of Venice
Must needs give sentence 'gainst the merchant there.

SHYLOCK My deeds upon my head! I crave the law,
The penalty and forfeit of my bond.

PORTIA Is he not able to discharge the money?

BASSANIO Yes, here I tender it for him in the court;
Yea, twice the sum: if that will not suffice,
I will be bound to pay it ten times o'er,
On forfeit of my hands, my head, my heart:
If this will not suffice, it must appear
That malice bears down truth. And I beseech you,
Wrest once the law to your authority:
To do a great right, do a little wrong,
And curb this cruel devil of his will.

PORTIA It must not be; there is no power in Venice
Can alter a decree established:
'Twill be recorded for a precedent,
And many an error by the same example
Will rush into the state: it cannot be.

SHYLOCK A Daniel come to judgment! yea, a Daniel!
O wise young judge, how I do honour thee!

PORTIA I pray you, let me look upon the bond.

SHYLOCK Here 'tis, most reverend doctor, here it is.

PORTIA Shylock, there's thrice thy money offer'd thee.

SHYLOCK An oath, an oath, I have an oath in heaven:
Shall I lay perjury upon my soul?
No, not for Venice.

PORTIA Why, this bond is forfeit;
And lawfully by this the Jew may claim
A pound of flesh, to be by him cut off
Nearest the merchant's heart. Be merciful:
Take thrice thy money; bid me tear the bond.

SHYLOCK When it is paid according to the tenor.
It doth appear you are a worthy judge;
You know the law, your exposition
Hath been most sound: I charge you by the law,
Whereof you are a well-deserving pillar,
Proceed to judgment: by my soul I swear
There is no power in the tongue of man
To alter me: I stay here on my bond.

ANTONIO Most heartily I do beseech the court
To give the judgment.

PORTIA Why then, thus it is:
You must prepare your bosom for his knife.

SHYLOCK O noble judge! O excellent young man!

PORTIA For the intent and purpose of the law
Hath full relation to the penalty,
Which here appeareth due upon the bond.

SHYLOCK 'Tis very true: O wise and upright judge!
How much more elder art thou than thy looks!

PORTIA Therefore lay bare your bosom.

SHYLOCK Ay, his breast:
So says the bond: doth it not, noble judge?
'Nearest his heart:' those are the very words.

PORTIA It is so. Are there balance here to weigh
The flesh?

SHYLOCK I have them ready.

PORTIA Have by some surgeon, Shylock, on your charge,
To stop his wounds, lest he do bleed to death.

SHYLOCK Is it so nominated in the bond?

PORTIA It is not so express'd: but what of that?
'Twere good you do so much for charity.

SHYLOCK I cannot find it; 'tis not in the bond.

PORTIA You, merchant, have you any thing to say?

ANTONIO But little: I am arm'd and well prepared.
Give me your hand, Bassanio: fare you well!
Grieve not that I am fallen to this for you;
For herein Fortune shows herself more kind
Than is her custom: it is still her use
To let the wretched man outlive his wealth,
To view with hollow eye and wrinkled brow
An age of poverty; from which lingering penance
Of such misery doth she cut me off.
Commend me to your honourable wife:
Tell her the process of Antonio's end;
Say how I loved you, speak me fair in death;
And, when the tale is told, bid her be judge
Whether Bassanio had not once a love.

	Repent but you that you shall lose your friend,
	And he repents not that he pays your debt;
	For if the Jew do cut but deep enough,
	I'll pay it presently with all my heart.
BASSANIO	Antonio, I am married to a wife
	Which is as dear to me as life itself;
	But life itself, my wife, and all the world,
	Are not with me esteem'd above thy life:
	I would lose all, ay, sacrifice them all
	Here to this devil, to deliver you.
PORTIA	Your wife would give you little thanks for that,
	If she were by, to hear you make the offer.
GRATIANO	I have a wife, whom, I protest, I love:
	I would she were in heaven, so she could
	Entreat some power to change this currish Jew.
NERISSA	'Tis well you offer it behind her back;
	The wish would make else an unquiet house.
SHYLOCK	These be the Christian husbands. I have a daughter;
	Would any of the stock of Barrabas
	Had been her husband rather than a Christian!
Aside	We trifle time: I pray thee, pursue sentence.
PORTIA	
	A pound of that same merchant's flesh is thine:
	The court awards it, and the law doth give it.
SHYLOCK	Most rightful judge!
PORTIA	And you must cut this flesh from off his breast:
	The law allows it, and the court awards it.
SHYLOCK	Most learned judge! A sentence! Come, prepare!

PORTIA   Tarry a little; there is something else.
This bond doth give thee here no jot of blood;
The words expressly are 'a pound of flesh:'
Take then thy bond, take thou thy pound of flesh;
But, in the cutting it, if thou dost shed
One drop of Christian blood, thy lands and goods
Are, by the laws of Venice, confiscate
Unto the state of Venice.

GRATIANO   O upright judge! Mark, Jew: O learned judge!

SHYLOCK   Is that the law?

PORTIA   Thyself shalt see the act:
For, as thou urgest justice, be assured
Thou shalt have justice, more than thou desirest.

GRATIANO   O learned judge! Mark, Jew: a learned judge!

SHYLOCK   I take this offer, then; pay the bond thrice
And let the Christian go.

BASSANIO   Here is the money.

PORTIA   Soft!
The Jew shall have all justice; soft! no haste:
He shall have nothing but the penalty.

GRATIANO   O Jew! an upright judge, a learned judge!

PORTIA   Therefore prepare thee to cut off the flesh.
Shed thou no blood, nor cut thou less nor more
But just a pound of flesh: if thou cut'st more
Or less than a just pound, be it but so much
As makes it light or heavy in the substance,
Or the division of the twentieth part
Of one poor scruple, nay, if the scale do turn
But in the estimation of a hair,
Thou diest and all thy goods are confiscate.

GRATIANO A second Daniel, a Daniel, Jew!
Now, infidel, I have you on the hip.

PORTIA Why doth the Jew pause? take thy forfeiture.

SHYLOCK Give me my principal, and let me go.

BASSANIO I have it ready for thee; here it is.

PORTIA He hath refused it in the open court:
He shall have merely justice and his bond.

GRATIANO A Daniel, still say I, a second Daniel!
I thank thee, Jew, for teaching me that word.

SHYLOCK Shall I not have barely my principal?

PORTIA Thou shalt have nothing but the forfeiture,
To be so taken at thy peril, Jew.

SHYLOCK Why, then the devil give him good of it!
I'll stay no longer question.

PORTIA Tarry, Jew:
The law hath yet another hold on you.
It is enacted in the laws of Venice,
If it be proved against an alien
That by direct or indirect attempts
He seek the life of any citizen,
The party 'gainst the which he doth contrive
Shall seize one half his goods; the other half
Comes to the privy coffer of the state;
And the offender's life lies in the mercy
Of the duke only, 'gainst all other voice.
In which predicament, I say, thou stand'st;
For it appears, by manifest proceeding,
That indirectly and directly too
Thou hast contrived against the very life
Of the defendant; and thou hast incurr'd

	The danger formerly by me rehearsed. Down therefore and beg mercy of the duke.
DUKE	That thou shalt see the difference of our spirits, I pardon thee thy life before thou ask it: For half thy wealth, it is Antonio's; The other half comes to the general state, Which humbleness may drive unto a fine.
PORTIA	Ay, for the state, not for Antonio.
SHYLOCK	Nay, take my life and all; pardon not that: You take my house when you do take the prop That doth sustain my house; you take my life When you do take the means whereby I live.
PORTIA	What mercy can you render him, Antonio?
GRATIANO	A halter gratis; nothing else, for God's sake.
ANTONIO	So please my lord the duke and all the court To quit the fine for one half of his goods, I am content; so he will let me have The other half in use, to render it, Upon his death, unto the gentleman That lately stole his daughter: Two things provided more, that, for this favour, He presently become a Christian; The other, that he do record a gift, Here in the court, of all he dies possess'd, Unto his son Lorenzo and his daughter.
DUKE	He shall do this, or else I do recant The pardon that I late pronounced here.
PORTIA	Art thou contented, Jew? what dost thou say?
SHYLOCK	I am content.
PORTIA	Clerk, draw a deed of gift.

SHYLOCK I pray you, give me leave to go from hence;
I am not well: send the deed after me,
And I will sign it.

DUKE Get thee gone, but do it.

Exit SHYLOCK
Exeunt DUKE and his train

BASSANIO Most worthy gentleman, I and my friend
Have by your wisdom been this day acquitted
Of grievous penalties; in lieu whereof,
Three thousand ducats, due unto the Jew,
We freely cope your courteous pains withal.

ANTONIO And stand indebted, over and above,
In love and service to you evermore.

PORTIA He is well paid that is well satisfied;
And I, delivering you, am satisfied
And therein do account myself well paid:
My mind was never yet more mercenary.
I pray you, know me when we meet again:
I wish you well, and so I take my leave.

BASSANIO Dear sir, of force I must attempt you further:
Take some remembrance of us, as a tribute,
Not as a fee: grant me two things, I pray you,
Not to deny me, and to pardon me.

PORTIA You press me far, and therefore I will yield.

To ANTONIO

Give me your gloves, I'll wear them for your sake;

To BASSANIO

And, for your love, I'll take this ring from you:
Do not draw back your hand; I'll take no more;
And you in love shall not deny me this.

BASSANIO   This ring, good sir, alas, it is a trifle!
I will not shame myself to give you this.

PORTIA   I will have nothing else but only this;
And now methinks I have a mind to it.

BASSANIO   There's more depends on this than on the value.
The dearest ring in Venice will I give you,
And find it out by proclamation:
Only for this, I pray you, pardon me.

PORTIA   I see, sir, you are liberal in offers.

BASSANIO   Good sir, this ring was given me by my wife;
And when she put it on, she made me vow
That I should neither sell nor give nor lose it.

PORTIA   That 'scuse serves many men to save their gifts.
An if your wife be not a mad-woman,
And know how well I have deserved the ring,
She would not hold out enemy for ever,
For giving it to me. Well, peace be with you!

Exeunt PORTIA and NERISSA

ANTONIO   My Lord Bassanio, let him have the ring:
Let his deservings and my love withal
Be valued against your wife's commandment.

BASSANIO   Go, Gratiano, run and overtake him;
Give him the ring, and bring him, if thou canst,
Unto Antonio's house: away! make haste.

Exit GRATIANO

Come, you and I will thither presently;
And in the morning early will we both
Fly toward Belmont: come, Antonio.

Exeunt

ACT IV SCENE II

The same. A street.

Enter PORTIA NERISSA and GRATIANO

GRATIANO	Fair sir, my Lord Bassanio upon more advice
	Hath sent you here this ring, and doth entreat
	Your company at dinner.
PORTIA	That cannot be:
	His ring I do accept most thankfully.
NERISSA	Sir, I would speak with you.
Aside to PORTIA	I'll see if I can get my husband's ring,
	Which I did make him swear to keep for ever.
PORTIA	Thou mayst, I warrant.
	We shall have old swearing
	That they did give the rings away to men;
	But we'll outface them, and outswear them too.
Aloud	Away! make haste: thou knowist where I will tarry.
NERISSA	Come, good sir.

Exeunt

ACT V SCENE I

Belmont. Avenue to PORTIA'S house.

Enter LORENZO, JESSICA, PORTIA and NERISSA

LORENZO Your husband is at hand; I hear his trumpet.

Enter BASSANIO, ANTONIO, GRATIANO, and their followers

PORTIA You are welcome home, my lord.

BASSANIO I thank you, madam. Give welcome to my friend.
This is the man, this is Antonio,
To whom I am so infinitely bound.

PORTIA You should in all sense be much bound to him.
For, as I hear, he was much bound for you.

ANTONIO No more than I am well acquitted of.

PORTIA Sir, you are very welcome to our house.

GRATIANO [To NERISSA] By yonder moon I swear you do me wrong;
In faith, I gave it to the judge's clerk.

PORTIA A quarrel, ho, already! what's the matter?

GRATIANO About a hoop of gold, a paltry ring
That she did give me, whose posy was
For all the world like cutler's poetry
Upon a knife, 'Love me, and leave me not.'

NERISSA You swore to me, when I did give it you,
That you would wear it till your hour of death
And that it should lie with you in your grave:
Gave it a judge's clerk! no, God's my judge,
The clerk will ne'er wear hair on's face that had it.

GRATIANO He will, an if he live to be a man.

NERISSA Ay, if a woman live to be a man.

GRATIANO Now, by this hand, I gave it to a youth,
The judge's clerk, that begg'd it as a fee:
I could not for my heart deny it him.

PORTIA You were to blame, I must be plain with you,
To part so slightly with your wife's first gift:
A thing stuck on with oaths upon your finger
And so riveted with faith unto your flesh.
I gave my love a ring and made him swear
Never to part with it; and here he stands;
I dare be sworn for him he would not leave it
Nor pluck it from his finger, for the wealth
That the world masters. Now, in faith, Gratiano,
You give your wife too unkind a cause of grief:
An 'twere to me, I should be mad at it.

BASSANIO [Aside] Why, I were best to cut my left hand off
And swear I lost the ring defending it.

GRATIANO My Lord Bassanio gave his ring away
Unto the judge that begg'd it and indeed
Deserved it too; and then the boy, his clerk,
That took some pains in writing, he begg'd mine;
And neither man nor master would take aught
But the two rings.

PORTIA What ring gave you my lord?
Not that, I hope, which you received of me.

BASSANIO If I could add a lie unto a fault,
I would deny it; but you see my finger
Hath not the ring upon it; it is gone.

PORTIA Even so void is your false heart of truth.
By heaven, I will ne'er come in your bed
Until I see the ring.

NERISSA Nor I in yours
Till I again see mine.

BASSANIO Sweet Portia,
If you did know to whom I gave the ring,
If you did know for whom I gave the ring
And would conceive for what I gave the ring
And how unwillingly I left the ring,
When nought would be accepted but the ring,
You would abate the strength of your displeasure.

PORTIA If you had known the virtue of the ring,
Or half her worthiness that gave the ring,
Or your own honour to contain the ring,
You would not then have parted with the ring.
Nerissa teaches me what to believe:
I'll die for't but some woman had the ring.

BASSANIO No, by my honour, madam, by my soul,
No woman had it, but a civil doctor,
Which did refuse three thousand ducats of me
And begg'd the ring; the which I did deny him
And suffer'd him to go displeased away;
Even he that did uphold the very life
Of my dear friend. What should I say, sweet lady?
I was enforced to send it after him;
I was beset with shame and courtesy;
My honour would not let ingratitude
So much besmear it. Pardon me, good lady;
For, by these blessed candles of the night,
Had you been there, I think you would have begg'd
The ring of me to give the worthy doctor.

PORTIA Let not that doctor e'er come near my house:
Since he hath got the jewel that I loved,
And that which you did swear to keep for me,
I will become as liberal as you;
I'll not deny him any thing I have,
No, not my body nor my husband's bed:

| | Now, by mine honour, which is yet mine own, |
| | I'll have that doctor for my bedfellow. |

NERISSA And I his clerk; therefore be well advised
How you do leave me to mine own protection.

GRATIANO Well, do you so; let not me take him, then;
For if I do, I'll mar the young clerk's pen.

ANTONIO I am the unhappy subject of these quarrels.

PORTIA Sir, grieve not you; you are welcome notwithstanding.

BASSANIO Portia, forgive me this enforced wrong;
Pardon this fault, and by my soul I swear
I never more will break an oath with thee.

ANTONIO I once did lend my body for his wealth;
Which, but for him that had your husband's ring,
Had quite miscarried: I dare be bound again,
My soul upon the forfeit, that your lord
Will never more break faith advisedly.

PORTIA Then you shall be his surety. Give him this
And bid him keep it better than the other.

ANTONIO Here, Lord Bassanio; swear to keep this ring.

BASSANIO By heaven, it is the same I gave the doctor!

PORTIA I had it of him: pardon me, Bassanio;
For, by this ring, the doctor lay with me.

NERISSA And pardon me, my gentle Gratiano;
For the doctor's clerk last night did lie with me.

GRATIANO What, are we cuckolds ere we have deserved it?

PORTIA Speak not so grossly. You are all amazed:
You shall find that Portia was the doctor,

	Nerissa there her clerk: Antonio, you are welcome;
	And I have better news in store for you
	Than you expect: three of your argosies
	Are richly come to harbour suddenly.
ANTONIO	I am dumb.
BASSANIO	Were you the doctor and I knew you not?
GRATIANO	Were you the clerk that is to make me cuckold?
NERISSA	Ay, but the clerk that never means to do it,
	Unless he live until he be a man.
BASSANIO	Sweet doctor, you shall be my bed-fellow:
	When I am absent, then lie with my wife.
ANTONIO	Sweet lady, you have given me life and living;
	For here I read for certain that my ships
	Are safely come to road.
PORTIA	How now, Lorenzo!
	My clerk hath some good comforts too for you.
NERISSA	Ay, and I'll give them him without a fee.
	There do I give to you and Jessica,
	From the rich Jew, a special deed of gift,
	After his death, of all he dies possess'd of.
LORENZO	Fair ladies, you drop manna in the way
	Of starved people.
PORTIA	It is almost morning,
	And yet I am sure you are not satisfied
	Of these events at full. Let us go in;
	And charge us there upon inter'gatories,
	And we will answer all things faithfully.
GRATIANO	Let it be so: the first inter'gatory
	That my Nerissa shall be sworn on is,

Whether till the next night she had rather stay,
Or go to bed now, being two hours to day:
But were the day come, I should wish it dark,
That I were couching with the doctor's clerk.
Well, while I live I'll fear no other thing
So sore as keeping safe Nerissa's ring.

Exeunt

Other Abridged Shakespeare Plays in the Series

Printed in Great Britain
by Amazon